Pearson Primary Progress and Assess

Year 6

Science

Assessment Guide

Deborah Herridge, Debbie Eccles and Tanya Shields

PEARSON

Published by Pearson Education Limited, 80 Strand, London, WC2R 0RL

www.pearsonschools.co.uk

Text © Pearson Education Limited 2016

Original illustrations © Pearson Education Limited 2010 / 2016
Cover illustration © Pearson Education Limited 2016

First published 2016

20 19 18 17 16
10 9 8 7 6 5 4 3 2 1

British Library Cataloguing in Publication Data
A catalogue record for this book is available from the British Library

ISBN 9780435173913

Printed in the UK by Ashford Colour Press

Acknowledgements
The publisher would like to thank the following for their kind permission to reproduce their photographs:

(Key: b-bottom; c-centre; l-left; r-right; t-top)

Y6 CLT-Cutsheet/ 123RF.com: (P30_c, P30_d, P30_h).
Imagemore Co., Ltd: (P30_a). **Shutterstock.com:** Zhukov Oleg (P30_g); Vitalii Hulai (P30_n); Tompet (P30_i); tanuha2001 (P30_o); photosync (P30_l); moomsabuy (P30_j); ievgen sosnytskyi (P30_k); Hintau Aliaksei (P30_q); Garsya (P30_e); Eric Isselee (P30_p, P30_f); defpicture (P30_m); cbpix (P30_b).
Sozaijiten: (P30_r)

All other images © Pearson Education

2

Contents

An introduction to assessment

Assessment is, of course, essential and it is something that teachers do instinctively on a day-to-day basis. Because of this, assessment comes in different forms and guises. Much assessment is ongoing and **formative** as it stems from observations and informs ongoing teaching and learning in the classroom. This kind of assessment is conducted by teachers and teaching assistants, as well as by children through peer and self-assessment. Rich questioning provides instantaneous feedback for teachers which can result in adjustments to short-term and medium-term planning. **Evidence** of independent practice, demonstrated in a variety of different ways, supports teachers with this type of assessment too.

Summative teacher assessment also serves a purpose, both nationally and locally. Whilst national summative assessments hold providers of education to account and provide a useful point of comparison, local summative assessments are useful in reviewing a child's ability to use and apply the knowledge and understanding they have accrued in their day-to-day learning. They provide a vital insight for teachers into whether children have mastered key topics and they also highlight where children may be having difficulty. They provide teachers with a useful opportunity to review what has been taught and to plan what needs to be addressed in future lessons.

So teaching influences assessment and assessment influences teaching. Indeed, assessment and the curriculum are inextricably linked; all assessment should support teachers in determining how well children have understood what they have been taught and should feed into the ongoing teaching and learning cycle.

In all cases, assessment should be purposeful and should prompt action. Throughout the year as we work with each child, we gain greater and more solid understanding of their abilities, their strengths and weaknesses. An assessment, no matter how good, is not the child. It should neither constrain expectations nor limit endeavours.

As such, the focus of the Progress and Assess summative assessments and the teaching guidance is to provide teachers with a set of tools to help them gather and understand evidence in order to support children in their learning. The next few sections of this guide will take you through the Progress and Assess tools available to download from ActiveLearn Primary for subscribers to Science Bug or Progress and Assess Science, or in the print version of this assessment guide.

Your science progression maps

What are the progression maps?

This assessment guide contains all of your Year 6 science progression maps. There is a progression map for each year group from Year 1 to Year 6.

The progression maps track objectives in science across a child's primary education. They list National Curriculum objectives, both knowledge and working scientifically, and preceding steps for each objective. They have been written by the Science Bug author team; Deborah Herridge, Senior Lecturer and Primary Science Leader for ITE at the University of Northumbria, Debbie Eccles, Primary Professional Development Lead for the STEM centre at MMU and Tanya Shields, Professional Development Leader for the National STEM Learning Network. All three are partners in *Primarily Science*.

Key features of the progression maps

The science progression maps separate out working scientifically skills and knowledge objectives. These areas are then broken down into topic areas so that teachers can quickly find the objectives they are looking for. These topic areas break down the National Curriculum into manageable steps.

The number of objectives listed within each topic area differs from year to year.

- Any text in bold has been taken directly from the 2014 National Curriculum in England.

- Any text not in bold represents a smaller step that helps children to build the required knowledge or skills they need by the end of the year, and helps you to check their progress along the way.

- For knowledge objectives, we reference Science Bug lesson plans within our progression maps too, so that you can see where key objectives are covered in Science Bug. They act as a point of reference if you subscribe to this service. We do not include references to Science Bug lesson plans for working scientifically skills as these are broader than knowledge objectives and so are covered across multiple Science Bug units.

- For some working scientifically skills, we have given an indication of what children who are exceeding ARE may be able to achieve to help you make some accurate assessments of the most able children's abilities.

How to use the progression maps

We recommend sticking a copy of each progression map in the back of each child's science book. Alternatively, you could keep a copy for each child in your assessment folder.

The progression maps can then be used to keep a record of how children are doing and where further support or extension may be required. You can choose how to do this, but we have provided a box within each objective cell to help. You may want to insert a tick, cross or circle to indicate when an objective has been achieved.

You can use these to support your formative and summative assessment.

Working Scientifically UKS2

Objective — General	Observing and measuring (and observing over time)	Comparative and fair tests	Identifying and classifying	Looking for naturally occurring patterns and relationships	Recording and reporting findings	Researching using secondary sources
Explore and talk about their own ideas.	Make their own decisions about what observations to make, what measurements to use and for how long to make them, and whether to repeat them.	Select and plan the most appropriate type of scientific enquiry to use to answer scientific questions.	Be able, independently, to use simple databases or keys to identify or classify living things, objects or events.	Identify patterns that might be found in the natural environment.	Decide how to record data from a choice of familiar approaches.	Recognise which secondary sources will be most useful to research their ideas and begin to separate opinion from fact.
Ask pertinent questions.	Choose the most appropriate equipment to make measurements and explain how to use it accurately.	Recognise when and how to set up comparative and fair tests and explain which variables need to be controlled and why.	Be able to discuss reasons why living things are placed in one group and not another.	Systematically investigate the relationship between phenomena, e.g. light and shadows.	Use relevant scientific language and illustrations to discuss, communicate and justify their scientific ideas and talk about how scientific ideas have developed over time.	Use secondary sources, e.g. internet links to research objects, events and phenomena that cannot be experienced in the classroom, e.g. planetary movements, animals from around the world.
Explore ideas and raise different kinds of questions about scientific phenomena.	Recognise that some measurements or observations may need to be repeated.	Be able to state clearly which is the change variable and which is the measurement variable in a fair test.	Suggest reasons for similarities and differences.	Look for different causal relationships in their data and identify evidence that refutes or supports their ideas.	Decide on the most appropriate method to present findings graphically, e.g. using a line graph or bar chart for different types of data.	Gather and record data to help in answering questions.
Refine a scientific question so that it can be tested.	Repeat observations or measurements appropriately.	Systematically identify the effect of changing one variable at a time.	Begin to understand that broad groupings, such as micro-organisms, plants and animals can be subdivided.	Analyse functions, relationships and interactions more systematically.	Justify what type of presentation is appropriate to use.	
Understand that some scientific questions cannot be answered by a particular investigation.	Be able to select appropriate ranges or intervals of measurements.	Recognise that some variables may be more significant than others in investigations.	Identify the positive aspects and limitations of some forms of classification.	Find out about how scientific ideas have changed and developed over time as new evidence is discovered, e.g. ideas about the solar system.	Explain findings using data to identify causal relationships.	

Works with Science Bug

7

Pearson Primary Progress and Assess
Science Progression Map

Child's name: _____

8

Objective — General	Observing and measuring (and observing over time)	Comparative and fair tests	Identifying and classifying	Looking for naturally occurring patterns and relationships	Recording and reporting findings	Researching using secondary sources
Be able to suggest changes to questions following collection/analysis of data.	Explain how repeating measurements impacts on data collection.	Be able to justify their choice of method as being appropriate to answer their investigative question.	Use and develop keys and other information records to identify, classify and describe living things and materials.	Recognise when evidence supports an idea or not.	Recording data and results of increasing complexity using scientific diagrams and labels, classification keys, tables, scatter graphs, bar and line graphs.	
Understand a range of enquiries can be used together to explore an answer to a question.	Recognise when measurements or data are unreliable and be able to take steps to improve this.	Be able to use their results to identify when further tests and observations might be needed.	Create more complex forms of classification tools, e.g. databases, branching keys.	Be able to identify and offer explanations for anomalous results.	Reporting and presenting findings from enquiries, including conclusions, causal relationships and explanations of and degree of trust in results, in oral and written forms such as displays and other presentations.	
Recognise key aspects of a scientific question.	Taking measurements, using a range of scientific equipment, with increasing accuracy and precision, taking repeat readings when appropriate.	Compare their own results with others' and suggest reasons why there may be differences.	Create and use a variety of sources to identify and classify living things, objects and phenomena.	Identifying scientific evidence that has been used to support or refute ideas or arguments.		
		Recognise the limitations of tests.				
		Planning different types of scientific enquiries to answer questions, including recognising and controlling variables where necessary.				

Pearson Primary Progress and Assess
Science Progression Map

Year 6
Working Scientifically

Child's name: _____

Objective	General	Observing and measuring (and observing over time)	Comparative and fair tests	Identifying and classifying	Looking for naturally occurring patterns and relationships	Recording and reporting findings	Researching using secondary sources
			Using test results to make predictions to set up further comparative and fair tests.				

Works with Science Bug

Pearson Primary Progress and Assess
Science Progression Map

Knowledge Year 6

	Biology			Physics	
Objective	**Animals, including humans**	**Evolution and inheritance**	**Living things and their habitats**	**Light**	**Electricity**
	Know that the human body contains organs. *Y6 OB L1*	Know that geological time spans millions of years. *Y6 EAI L1*	Recognise common observable characteristics that can be used to group/classify living things. *Y6 CLT L1*	Know that light comes from a source and be able to name some sources of light. *Y6 LS L1*	Explore and describe how to construct circuits with a very dim bulb and others with very quiet buzzers. *Y6 CC L2, L3*
	Know that each organ has a specific function. *Y6 OB L1*	Know that some living things that were on Earth millions of years ago, e.g. dinosaurs, are no longer inhabiting Earth. They are extinct. *Y6 EAI L1*	Know that germs and bacteria are living organisms called micro-organisms. *Y6 CLT L2*	Know that light can travel from a source. *Y6 LS L1*	**Associate the brightness of a lamp or the volume of a buzzer with the number and voltage of cells used in the circuit.** *Y6 CC L2, L3*
	Know that the heart is the organ that pumps blood around the body through blood vessels. *Y6 OB L1*	Understand that evolution is the process of change in living things over time. *Y6 EAI L1, L2*	Understand that micro-organisms form part of the classification system for living things. *Y6 CLT L2*	Know that light can be reflected from shiny surfaces and be able to name some reflectors. *Y6 LS L1*	Explore the variation in how different electrical components function, constructing different circuits and describing findings. *Y6 CC L2, L3, L4*
	Understand that organs can also work together as a body 'system'. *Y6 OB L1, L2*	Understand that some fossils are examples of living things that were once alive on Earth but are no longer living. *Y6 EAI L1*	Identify the conditions needed to support the growth of micro-organisms. *Y6 CLT L3*	Notice how light from a source such as a torch travels. *Y6 LS L2*	**Compare and give reasons for variations in how components function, including the brightness of bulbs, the loudness of buzzers and the on/off position of switches.** *Y6 CC L2, L3, L4, L5*
	Know that together the heart, blood vessels and blood form the circulatory system. *Y6 OB L2*	Know that humans are a relatively recent species on Earth. *Y6 EAI L1*	**Describe how living things are classified into broad groups according to common observable characteristics and based on similarities and differences, including micro-organisms, plants and animals.** *Y6 CLT L1, L2, L3, L6*	Recognise that light appears to travel in straight lines. *Y6 LS L2*	Understand the need for universally recognised symbols for electrical components. *Y6 CC L1*

Key to Science Bug units: CLT: Classifying Living Things, CC: Changing Circuits,

Pearson Primary Progress and Assess
Science Progression Map

Child's name: _____

Objective	Animals, including humans	Evolution and inheritance	Living things and their habitats	Light	Electricity
	Understand that blood picks up oxygen from the lungs and transports it through blood vessels to all of our organs. Y6 OB L2	**Recognise that living things have changed over time and that fossils provide information about living things that inhabited the Earth millions of years ago.** Y6 EAI L1	Know that there is a scientific system for classifying living things. Y6 CLT L4	Know that without light we cannot see. Y6 LS L3	Identify recognised electrical component symbols for a bulb, buzzer, battery (cell), wire, switch and motor. Y6 CC L2
	Identify and name the main parts of the human circulatory system, and describe the functions of the heart, blood vessels and blood. Y6 OB L1, L2, L3, L6	Know that living things reproduce offspring similar to themselves. Y6 EAI L2	Identify the observable characteristics used to identify local plants. Y6 CLT L4, L5	Understand that an object can be seen when it gives out or reflects light into our eyes. Y6 LS L3, L5	**Use recognised symbols when representing a simple circuit in a diagram.** Y6 CC L1, L2, L3, L6
	Know that humans need water and food to survive. Y6 OB L2	Understand that offspring will bear some similarities to each other, to their parents and to other living things of the same kind. Y6 EAI L2	Identify the observable characteristics to classify a specific species of plant, e.g. a buttercup. Y6 CLT L5	**Use the idea that light travels in straight lines to explain that objects are seen because they give out or reflect light into the eye.** Y6 LS L3, L4, L5	
	Know that the substances in food that help us to grow and repair our bodies are termed 'nutrients'. Y6 OB L1, L2	Recognise that small inherited changes in physical characteristics, e.g. colour, size, shape of limbs etc. over time lead to variation in species. Y6 EAI L2	Identify the observable characteristics to classify a specific species of animal, e.g. an earthworm. Y6 CLT L6	Know that light can be reflected from surfaces. Y6 LS L4	
	Understand that it is the circulatory system that transports water and nutrients around our bodies. Y6 OB L1, L2	**Recognise that living things produce offspring of the same kind, but normally offspring vary and are not identical to their parents.** Y6 EAI L2, L3	**Give reasons for classifying plants and animals based on specific characteristics.** Y6 CLT L1, L4, L5, L6	Know that different surfaces reflect light in different ways. Y6 LS L4	
	Describe the ways in which nutrients and water are transported within animals, including humans. Y6 OB L2, L3	Know that animals and plants exist and live in different environments. Y6 EAI L3		Know that light is more scattered when it is reflected off a dull surface. Y6 LS L4	
	Know that body systems respond to a person's physical needs, e.g. to run faster, to digest food. Y6 OB L3, L4, L5	Know that not all animals or plants will survive to reproduce. Y6 EAI L3		Know that smooth and shiny surfaces reflect light well. Y6 LS L4	

Key to Science Bug units: CLT: Classifying Living Things, CC: Changing Circuits, LS: Light and Sight, OB: Our Bodies, EAI: Evolution and Inheritance

Works with Science Bug

Pearson Primary Progress and Assess
Science Progression Map

Child's name: _____

Year 6
Knowledge

12

	Animals, including humans	Evolution and inheritance	Living things and their habitats	Light	Electricity
Objective	Understand that some aspects of a person's lifestyle, e.g. lack of exercise, taking narcotics, will have an effect on the way their body functions. *Y6 OB L4, L5, L6*	Understand that variation in offspring over time can make animals and plants more or less able to survive in particular environments. *Y6 EAI L3, L4, L5*		Explain that we see things because light travels from light sources to our eyes or from light sources to objects and then to our eyes. *Y6 LS L1*	
	Recognise the impact of diet, exercise, drugs and lifestyle on the way their bodies function. *Y6 OB L4, L5, L6*	Know that some adaptations to the environment in plants or animals can be advantageous if they keep the species alive for long enough to reproduce and pass on their features to a new generation. *Y6 EAI L4, L5*		Understand that light travels in straight lines. *Y6 LS L2*	
		Know that living things start from a common ancestor but have evolved to suit the environmental conditions. *Y6 EAI L4, L5*		Know that light cannot travel around objects. *Y6 LS L6*	
		Identify how animals and plants are adapted to suit their environment in different ways and that adaptation may lead to evolution. *Y6 EAI L4, L5, L6*		Know that some materials let light pass through them. *Y6 LS L6*	
				Understand that light is blocked by opaque materials. *Y6 LS L6*	
				Understand that when opaque materials block the path of light a shadow can be cast. *Y6 LS L6*	
				Know that shadows are similar in shape to the objects which make them. *Y6 LS L6*	

Key to Science Bug units: CLT: Classifying Living Things, CC: Changing Circuits,

© Pearson Education Ltd 2015

Pearson Primary Progress and Assess
Science Progression Map

Child's name: _____

Objective	Animals, including humans	Evolution and inheritance	Living things and their habitats	Light	Electricity
				Use the idea that light travels in straight lines to explain why shadows have the same shape as the objects that cast them. *Y6 LS L6*	

Key to Science Bug units: CLT: Classifying Living Things, CC: Changing Circuits, LS: Light and Sight, OB: Our Bodies, EAI: Evolution and Inheritance

Works with Science Bug

The science summative assessments

About the summative assessments

The summative assessments are optional and can be used if you feel you do not have enough formative assessments to make a judgment on children's attainment. They are intended to be an addition to your formative assessment. They are available in the printed assessment guides as photocopiables. If you subscribe to Science Bug or Progress and Assess Science, you can also download the summative assessments from ActiveLearn Primary.

We provide six summative assessments per year with the intention of one being used at the end of each half term. Please note that there are five assessments in Year 6 rather than six because of SATs in the summer term. Before using a summative assessment with your class, it is important that you check to see that you have taught the objectives that are being assessed. You can use the progression maps to help you do this. The summative assessments do not have to be covered in any particular order and can fit in with the order that you teach the different science topics.

Each summative assessment covers both knowledge National Curriculum objectives and working scientifically skills. Therefore, they have both a written and practical element.

Supporting documents

There are a number of resources which support the summative assessments.

- Teacher guidance specific to each summative assessment. This contains an explanation of what's covered in each summative assessment, what needs to be prepared in advance of children doing the activity and the National Curriculum objectives being assessed (separated out into knowledge and working scientifically). The teacher guidance also contains a best fit marking guidance grid which gives detailed advice on making attainment judgments for knowledge objectives and working scientifically skills. The teacher guidance is available to download from ActiveLearn Primary as a linked resource accompanying each summative assessment.

- Optional writing frames have been provided to capture children's written work and support children in their writing. Not all summative assessments require children to create a structured piece of writing so these summative assessments do not have a writing frame.

Using the summative assessments with your class

Before using the summative assessments with your class, it is important that you check to see that you have taught the objectives that are being assessed.

- These summative assessments can be used with the whole class or groups of children.

- Print a summative assessment sheet and writing frame (where applicable) for each child in your class or group and hand them out.

- If you choose to use a writing frame, children should write their name, class and the date at the top.

- Ensure children have the resources they need to complete the summative assessment. Resources and equipment children will need for each summative assessment is listed on each teacher guidance document.

- Lead the assessment activity in the same way you would deliver a lesson. There is no time limit for the assessment activity but we recommend allowing about two hours. It is important that children have enough time to demonstrate what they can do. Teachers should adjust this time depending on the needs of their class or group and should decide whether children require breaks throughout the session.

- Talk through the 'What you need to do' section of the assessment and read out the words they may find helpful given at the bottom of each summative assessment sheet.

Making an attainment judgment

General tips

Once children have completed a summative assessment, it is good practice to review the activity and use your insights to define future learning needs for different children.

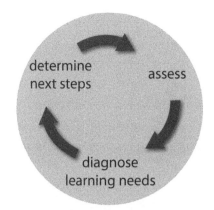

When making attainment judgments, it is important to refer to the marking guidance grid on the second page of the teacher guidance document, available online as a linked resource accompanying each summative assessment.

How to use the teacher guidance documents

Teacher guidance documents are available to accompany each summative assessment.

The first page of the teacher guidance documents explain what is covered in the assessment, what needs to be prepared in advance of children doing the activity and the National Curriculum objectives being assessed.

The second page of the Teacher Guidance is the best fit marking guidance grid. There is detailed guidance on deciding whether pupil's knowledge and working scientifically skills Exceed ARE, are On Track for ARE, or Working Towards ARE. You will also be able to classify children's attainment as Below ARE if you feel they are not coming under as Working Towards ARE. The advice provided within the best fit marking guidance grids is informed by the progression map.

The Teacher Guidance documents are available on ActiveLearn Primary as linked resources to each assessment and within the printed Assessment Guides.

Recording and understanding attainment

If you subscribe to Science Bug, or Progress and Assess Science, you can input your attainment judgments directly into ActiveLearn Primary. You can find out more about how to do this in our getting started guide.

The attainment judgments for knowledge and working scientifically should be considered alongside your knowledge of the child and your formative judgments.

Feeding back to children

Feeding back to children is an important part of the assessment cycle. You can record individual attainment judgments and feedback in the space provided at the end of the writing frame.

Remember to provide feedback on what children did well, as well as areas they can continue to improve. Make learning targets specific and achievable, and ensure you have a plan in place to support children with strengthening and extending their learning. Plan feedback conversations and think carefully about how you can present this information to children.

What went well	
How to improve	

Feeding back to parents

It can be useful to report results to parents too, to inform them about their child's achievement across a period of time. Make sure you check your assessment policy, as it may contain useful information on how to approach this. Think carefully about how you communicate attainment judgments; how, for example, you can communicate that a child working below ARE is actually doing quite well.

Feeding back to other stakeholders

Local summative assessment will not provide a comparison between schools, so think about what information stakeholders need to see and how this should be presented.

Snow blind

Teacher Guidance

Light and Sight

NC objectives

K: Explain that we see things because light travels from light sources to our eyes or from light sources to objects and then to our eyes.

WS: Planning different types of scientific enquiries to answer questions, including recognising and controlling variables where necessary.

Overview

Children will apply knowledge about how we see, and how light travels and is reflected, to a modern day application.

Key concepts

- Reflection
- How light travels

Resources / equipment

- Torches and other strong light sources
- A variety of sunglasses labelled with letters
- White card and black card
- Data loggers
- An optional writing frame has been provided for this assessment activity.

Outcomes

- Children write an explanation of how light is reflected from surfaces into our eyes so we can see.
- They explain why we need to protect our eyes from strong sunlight.

Teaching notes

- Introduce the assessment activity by asking children to think about being outside when it has just snowed or being on a winter sports holiday. Discuss how bright it can appear when snow has just fallen.
- *What do you think happens when moonlight reflects off snow? Is it still bright?* (Yes) Remind children that the Moon is not a light source, it is just reflecting the light of the Sun so it is actually a double reflection of light. Remind children that light travels in straight lines and when it hits a surface it is reflected (to a greater or lesser degree). When the reflected light hits our eyes then we can see.
- During the day, sunlight hits the surface of white snow and the snow actually increases the total amount of sunlight reflecting back to the eyes (when compared to ground without snow). Talk about how we need to protect our eyes from excessively strong sunlight.
- Explain that the snow isn't producing extra light it is just reflecting light from the Sun. Snow reflects light so well that people can get what is called 'snow blindness'. The light is so bright that the contrast of moving from inside to outside is so much that it takes a while for our eyes to adjust to the different light levels so we can see.
- Set up a demonstration using a data logger (or have children do this themselves if you have enough equipment) to explore the differences in reflected light from a white or a dark surface (to model snow-covered and snow-free ground). Explore the effects of placing sunglasses in front of the light sensor on the data logger. Discuss the effects. Ensure the sunglasses are labelled with a letter for clarity when referring to them.
- Draw a generic diagram of the path of light from a light source to an object and then into our eyes. Explain that children will write a paragraph for a product report on sunglasses, specifically explaining how light from the Sun behaves when it hits snow and why the team should wear sunglasses. Including a diagram of how light travels might make it easier to explain.

	Knowledge	Working Scientifically
Exceeding ARE	Recognise simple patterns in the data they have collected and be able to predict not yet known values from the patterns of their results. Able to explain how light travels in straight lines from a source and is reflected in terms of the journey of light from source to eye. Able to represent and explain this path using accurate diagrams.	Describe or identify evidence which supports or disproves scientific ideas, e.g. do pale colours always reflect light better than dark colours? Suggest reasons for limitations or inconsistencies in results from investigations and decide how these may impact on their conclusions. Refine a scientific question and test it. Compare their own results with others and suggest reasons why there may be differences.
On track for ARE	Able to explain that light travels in straight lines from a source where it enters the eye causing images to be seen. Able to describe and explain how objects and shiny surfaces can reflect light. Able to plan and carry out an investigation into which material reflects most light and report on their findings. Able to represent their ideas in drawings and diagrams.	Explore ideas and raise different kinds of questions about scientific phenomena. Refine a scientific question so that it can be tested. Understand a range of enquiries can be used together to explore an answer to a question. Record data and results of increasing complexity using scientific diagrams and labels, classification keys, tables, scatter graphs, bar and line graphs. Recognise some limitations of tests.
Working towards ARE	Understand that light travels in straight lines but that it can be reflected and change direction. Understand that we need light to see and that when light is blocked a shadow is formed. Able to describe and explain the results of their investigations in simple terms.	Explore and talk about their own ideas. Recognise connections between their original question, the results of their enquiry and whether they can answer the question.

N.B. Any children not hitting *working towards ARE* should come under *below ARE* when recording attainment in Active Learn Primary.

Pearson Primary Progress and Assess © Pearson Education Ltd 2015

Snow blind!

The Winter Olympic ski team are testing a new brand of sunglasses. They need help to convince their coach that they need high quality sunglasses.

Can you help them?

> **What you need to do**
> - You are the science consultant on the project.
> - Write a paragraph for the final product report explaining why the team need to wear sunglasses and how light from the Sun behaves when it hits snow.
> - Include diagrams in your report.

> **You may find these words helpful**
> straight lines, the Sun, travel, reflect, surface, light, see, scatter, white

Name: _____

Class: _____ **Date:** _____

Product report: sunglasses

How light from the Sun behaves when it hits snow:

_____

_____

_____

Diagram:

The team should wear sunglasses because:

_____

_____

_____

For teacher use

What went well	
How to improve	

Healthy hearts

Teacher Guidance

NC objectives

K: Identify and name the main parts of the human circulatory system, and describe the functions of the heart, blood vessels and blood.

WS: Identifying scientific evidence that has been used to support or refute ideas or arguments.

Overview

Children will research evidence on heart health and will write a report on the importance of a healthy heart and its function and role in maintaining a healthy body.

Key concepts

- Healthy living
- Heart and the circulatory system
- Importance and impact of diet and exercise on the body

Resources / equipment

- Access to the internet and library books for research
- Examples of fitness DVDs or fitness adverts
- An optional writing frame has been provided for this assessment activity.

Outcomes

- Children write a guide about keeping the heart healthy and other aspects of healthy living.

Teaching notes

- Remind children briefly of all they have learned about keeping their bodies healthy.
- Read the scenario of the assessment activity together. *How do you think weight and a healthy heart could be linked?* (Link heart health to improved stamina, more efficient circulation, being better able to exercise and so having leaner bodies.)
- Suggest that sometimes people do not want to recognise that advice they are given on keeping healthy is correct, e.g. many people who know the risks of smoking or drinking too much don't cut their consumption and lots of people do no exercise at all.
- Ask children how scientists might be able to better persuade people of health messages, e.g. research studies with strong evidence of outcomes.
- *Where can we find the evidence to support the ideas of keeping healthy and heart health?* (Reputable books and websites)
- Ask children to do some research on healthy living and heart health and to write a section of a guide to leading a healthy lifestyle. Ensure children have access to the internet and library resources in the classroom. Ask them to concentrate on keeping the heart healthy and to suggest reasons why this might impact on overall health.

22

	Knowledge	Working Scientifically
Exceeding ARE	Able to recognise the interdependent nature of the different systems of the body. Able to describe and explain the function of the heart and circulatory system in detail, e.g. that blood picks up oxygen from the lungs and transports it through blood vessels to all of our organs. Able to link the function of the heart and the circulatory system to overall health. Able to recognise the impact of diet, exercise and drugs on the way their bodies function and able to communicate this in a number of different ways.	Able to draw conclusions from data they have collected through investigations and research, and evaluate the value of this. Be able to identify and offer explanations for anomalous results that they find in the data from secondary sources.
On track for ARE	Able to identify the main parts of the human circulatory system and able to describe the functions of the heart, blood vessels and blood. Able to describe how water and nutrients are transported throughout the body and know the effect of exercise on pulse rates. Able to recognise the impact of diet, exercise and drugs on the way their bodies function and able to communicate this information in a number of different ways.	Identify patterns that might be found in the natural environment, e.g. between exercise and pulse rate. Look for different causal relationships in their data and identify evidence that refutes or supports their ideas. Recognise when evidence supports or does not support an idea. Identify scientific evidence that has been used to support or refute ideas or arguments.
Working towards ARE	Understand that blood circulates through the human body and is pumped by the heart. Recognise that they need a balance of food and exercise to stay healthy. Able to understand that alcohol, tobacco and drugs can have a detrimental effect on their health.	Use information from secondary sources to help answer a question. Identify relevant evidence used to draw conclusions. Use straightforward scientific evidence to answer questions or to support their findings.

N.B. Any children not hitting *working towards ARE* should come under *below ARE* when recording attainment in Active Learn Primary.

Healthy hearts

Fitness instructor Toni McKay is the presenter of Channel 9's new diet, fitness and lifestyle show *Healthy Hearts!* She is helping Vicky and Ted to lead healthier lives.

What can Vicky and Ted do to improve their heart health?

What you need to do

- Toni gives each contestant a healthy lifestyle guide.
- She thinks Vicky and Ted need to improve their heart health.
- Write a section of the guide about what the heart does and why it's important.
- What other advice should Toni give to Vicky and Ted on how to stay fit and healthy?

You may find these words helpful

heart, muscle, pulse rate, circulate, blood, oxygen, diet, exercise, healthy, unhealthy, moderate, drugs, alcohol, smoking, tobacco, fruit, vegetables, calories, weight, balance

Name: _____

Class: _____ **Date:** _____

A guide to keeping the heart healthy

What does the heart do and how does it work?

_____

_____

_____

Diagram:

Tips for keeping your heart healthy:

• _____

• _____

Further advice on keeping fit and healthy:

• _____

• _____

For teacher use

What went well	
How to improve	

Classification chaos

Teacher Guidance

NC objectives

K: Give reasons for classifying plants and animals based on specific characteristics.
WS: Recording data and results of increasing complexity using scientific diagrams and labels, classification keys, tables, scatter graphs, bar and line graphs.

Overview

Children will classify living things and sort them into matching pairs. They will write the instructions and answers for a classification card game.

Key concepts

- Grouping
- Identifying
- Classifying

Resources / equipment

- Scissors
- Pencils
- Colouring pencils
- Card for children to create their own cards
- Cards from cut sheet, one set per child (either prepare these before the session or give each child a cut sheet)
- An optional writing frame has been provided for this assessment activity.

Outcomes

- Children produce hints, tips and instructions for identifying living things.
- They create living things cards to be added to a deck of cards.

Teaching notes

- Set the scene for the assessment activity by explaining Miss Abram's problem. She has a classification card game but the instructions have gone missing. *Can you help to write a new set of instructions?*
- You may need to explain how to play pairs before children begin the activity. Explain that a set of cards are laid face down and each player takes it in turns to turn over two cards. If they find a matching pair they get to keep the cards. If they fail to find a matching pair they place the cards back face down. The winner of the game is the person who finds the most pairs.
- Display a selection of the cards for the whole class to see, e.g. tulip, bacteria, fox and fish. Ask children to suggest some of the classification groups they could use to identify the pairs, e.g. micro-organisms, plants, mammals, fish. Explain that there are ten different pairs within the pack of cards.
- Ask children to use the cards from the cut sheet to identify all nine pairs before writing the instructions and answer sheet. Either prepare the cards for each child before the session or allow children time to cut the cards out themselves.
- Children then identify and create new cards that could be added to the pack.
- If time permits, children can play the game using their new cards. They could also think of different rules to simplify the game for young children, e.g. using simpler classification systems such as living and non-living, plants and animals.

26

Classification chaos
Teacher Guidance

	Knowledge	Working Scientifically
Exceeding ARE	Use correct scientific vocabulary to classify living things, e.g. plants, animals, micro-organisms. Can independently identify a range of sub-groups within plants and animals, e.g. animals – reptiles, mammals, birds, fish, amphibians, and can give examples of animals which belong to each sub-group. Accurately describe how living things are classified based on observable characteristics and may identify characteristics that are not observable, e.g. mammals are warm-blooded, reptiles are cold-blooded.	Accurately identify and classify a range of living things. Can independently create complex identification keys using scientific criteria, e.g. does the animal have gills, feathers, scales?
On track for ARE	Describe how living things are classified into broad groups according to common observable characteristics and based on similarities and differences, including micro-organisms, plants and animals, e.g. mammals have fur, reptiles have scaly skin, birds have wings.	Use and develop keys and other information records to identify, classify and describe living things. Can describe similarities and differences, e.g. fish live in the sea, mammals live on land. Begin to understand that broad groupings, such as micro-organisms, plants and animals can be sub-divided.
Working towards ARE	Can identify similarities and differences between living things, e.g. has wings, doesn't have wings, lives in the sea, doesn't live in the sea. Can identify some of the scientific names for the different sub-groups.	Can group animals according to similarities and differences and, with support, can classify animals into scientifically recognised sub-groups, e.g. it has feathers so it is a bird.

N.B. Any children not hitting *working towards ARE* should come under *below ARE* when recording attainment in Active Learn Primary.

27

Classification chaos

Miss Abrams has found a classification card game to play with her class. Unfortunately, the instructions have gone missing.

Can you write a set of instructions that explain how to play the game?
You will need to include an answer sheet that explains which cards form pairs and why.

What you need to do
- Look at the different cards in the pack. Identify which cards make a matching pair.
- Write a set of instructions to explain how to play the game. Include a set of answers explaining why certain cards make a pair.
- Create some new cards for the pack.

You may find these words helpful
flowering, non-flowering, plants, reptile, fish, bird, insect, minibeast, amphibian, micro-organism, not living, living

Classification chaos

Name:

Class: _____ **Date:** _____

How to play classification pairs

Instructions

	Answers	
Pair 1	and	because...
Pair 2	and	because...
Pair 3	and	because...
Pair 4	and	because...
Pair 5	and	because...
Pair 6	and	because...
Pair 7	and	because...
Pair 8	and	because...
Pair 9	and	because...

For teacher use

What went well	
How to improve	

tulip | shark | bacteria | oak tree

moss | cow | rabbit | dolphin

cat | mould | fern | whale

crocodile | newt | fish | fox

frog | snake

Dim and dimmer
Teacher Guidance

NC objectives

K: Associate the brightness of a lamp or the volume of a buzzer with the number and voltage of cells used in the circuit.

K: Compare and give reasons for variations in how components function, including the brightness of bulbs, the loudness of buzzers and the on/off position of switches.

WS: Reporting and presenting findings from enquiries, including conclusions, causal relationships and explanations of and degree of trust in results, in oral and written forms such as displays and other presentations.

Overview

Children will carry out an investigation to find out what affects the brightness of a bulb and the volume of a buzzer in a circuit.

Key concepts

- Reporting findings
- Causal relationships
- Problem solving

Resources / equipment

- A computer/data logger with light sensor
- Fuse wire (nichrome)
- A metre rule
- Batteries of different voltages
- Bulbs of different types
- Connecting wire with crocodile clips
- Copper wire
- Graphite rods
- A 60 cm long balsa wood board with a screw at each end to hold the different wires (to change the length of the wire, move crocodile clips along it)
- Paper for presenting findings.

Outcomes

- Children present a solution to the problem of needing dimmer lights and a louder buzzer in a house.

31

Teaching notes

- Set the scene for the assessment activity by explaining that Mrs Clarke's mother has difficulty hearing her door buzzer and suffers from migraines so needs dimmer lights in her house. They will be investigating how to make a buzzer as loud as possible and how to make a bulb as dim as possible.
- Show children the electrical components and explain that they are going to explore using these in helping to dim the lights and increase the volume of the buzzer.
- *How do you think you could change the brightness of the bulb and the loudness of a buzzer in a circuit?* Accept suggestions for changing the number of cells or bulbs/buzzers but encourage other possibilities such as wire length/type.
- Explain that children will share their results with the rest of the class so they need to present their findings clearly.
- Encourage systematic recording of their results which can also include circuit diagrams.
- *Can you explain what is happening to the current in the circuit and why the bulb grows dimmer?*
- Discuss other household appliances where we need to vary the output, e.g. volume controls on radios.
- Please note that a writing frame has not been provided for this assessment activity as children should select their own way of presenting their findings.

Dim and dimmer
Teacher Guidance

	Knowledge	Working Scientifically
Exceeding ARE	Able to give more complex explanations for altering bulb brightness and volume of a buzzer relating to both voltage and resistance, e.g. can state that the bulb is dimmer when attached to a longer length of fuse wire as it resists the flow of electricity.	Able to present reasoned explanation, e.g. uses models and analogies related to resistance and voltage to explain dimmer bulbs and a louder buzzer.
On track for ARE	Able to associate the brightness of a lamp or the volume of a buzzer with the voltage of cells used in the circuit, e.g. during the presentation outlines how using different voltage batteries will alter the volume of the buzzer or brightness of a bulb. Able to compare and give reasons for how components function, including the brightness of bulbs, the loudness of buzzers and the on/off position of switches.	Able to report and present findings from enquiries, including conclusions, causal relationships and in oral and written forms such as displays and other presentations, e.g. gives a presentation that includes reasonable solutions to dimming bulbs and increasing volume of the buzzer such as using longer fuse wire in the circuit including the bulb and using additional cells in the circuit including the buzzer.
Working towards ARE	Able to get a bulb to light and a buzzer to sound by making a complete circuit.	Able to describe their observations from investigating altering the brightness of bulbs or volume of a buzzer, e.g. recalls that different batteries meant the bulb lit up to different degrees.

N.B. Any children not hitting *working towards ARE* should come under *below ARE* when recording attainment in Active Learn Primary.

Dim and dimmer

Mrs Clarke's class are trying to solve a problem.

They have been asked to find a way to help Mrs Clarke's mother who has poor hearing and suffers with migraines. They need to work out how to make the doorbell buzzer louder and the lights dimmer.

Can you help them?

What you need to do
- Use the equipment to investigate how to make the buzzer as loud as possible and the light bulb as dim as possible.
- Present your results.

You may find these words helpful

circuit, nichrome wire, battery, cell, circuit diagram, resistance, bulb, buzzer, component

---

Now you see me, now you don't!

Teacher Guidance

NC objectives

K: Identify how animals and plants are adapted to suit their environment in different ways and that adaptation may lead to evolution.

WS: Identifying scientific evidence that has been used to support or refute ideas or arguments.

Overview

Children will carry out a challenge to model natural selection through the example of the peppered moth.

Key concepts

- Natural selection
- Adaptation
- Camouflage

Resources / equipment

- Internet access or access to library resources for research
- Black paper
- Pages of newsprint photocopied onto white paper
- Small 1cm cut-outs of moth shapes in both black paper and newsprint paper
- Plastic tweezers
- Safety goggles misted with petroleum jelly
- Stopwatch
- An optional writing frame has been provided for this assessment activity.

Outcomes

- Children research and model evolution over a short period using the example of the peppered moth.
- They write an explanation of how inherited features can lead to competitive advantage and evolution.

Teaching notes

- Remind children of the ideas of Charles Darwin that life on Earth has changed slowly over time and living things have gradually adapted to suit their environment. Explain that the peppered moth is a relatively modern example of evolution where a species which was very short-lived changed to suit its environment in just a few generations, over 50 years rather than hundreds of thousands of years.
- Peppered moths were normally white with black speckles and they were hidden against white lichens on trees. There was also a naturally black mutation of the moth that stood out against trees and was easily spotted and eaten by birds. They did not survive to breed so were in the minority. However, in the 19th century, pollution blackened the trees and killed the pale lichens. The black moth survived to reproduce whereas the pale moth was eaten. In just a few years environmental conditions had changed and the moths had evolved by natural selection into a mostly black species.
- Explain that children are going to model this change in competitive advantage by completing a challenge. They will be birds seeking out moths for food. To make it more challenging they will wear misted goggles to simulate how a bird might focus in flight. Put a large number of newsprint peppered moths on a newsprint background. *How many peppered moths can you pick up with tweezers in 30 seconds?* Try again using black moths on the newsprint background. *How many this time?* Now mix them together on the newsprint background. *What do you notice? Do you find the black moths first?* Introduce and explain the term 'camouflage'.
- Change the background to black to represent soot-covered trees. *Which moth is easiest to see? Which will be eaten? Which will survive to reproduce and pass its features on?*
- Ask children to write a paragraph on what the example of the peppered moth shows us about how evolution develops through natural selection. Then ask them to choose another animal they are familiar with that has clear physical adaptations and to explain how the adaptation gives the chosen animal a competitive advantage in the wild. Allow children access to the internet or information books to complete this task.

Now you see me, now you don't!
Teacher Guidance

	Knowledge	Working Scientifically
Exceeding ARE	Able to confidently explain the theories of evolution by means of natural selection and able to describe examples of this and able to provide evidence in support of these theories. Know that the fossil record and isolated habitats provide evidence in support of this theory. Able to identify beneficial adaptations in existing living things which may lead to evolution.	Describe evidence both from secondary sources and from the different causal relationships they have identified in their data which supports or refutes accepted or developing ideas. Identify possible flaws in arguments and distinguish confidently between fact and opinion.
On track for ARE	Able to describe how evolution by means of natural selection occurs over time. Relate this to more modern examples of inheritance and selective breeding in, for example, dogs. Able to describe the life stories and discoveries of key scientists in the field of evolutionary biology. Recognise that small inherited changes in physical characteristics, e.g. colour, size, shape of limbs etc. over time leads to variation in species.	Identify patterns that might be found in the natural environment. Systematically investigate the relationship between phenomena and natural environment, e.g. effects of camouflage. Look for different causal relationships in their data and identify evidence that refutes or supports their ideas from secondary sources. Identify scientific evidence that has been used to support or refute ideas or arguments. Find out about how scientific ideas have changed and developed over time as new evidence is discovered, e.g. ideas about evolution.
Working towards ARE	Understand that there were animals alive on Earth many millions of years ago that no longer exist and be able to name examples of these. Recognise that animals are suited to the environments in which they live.	Recognise links between observations and answers to questions. Use patterns in their data to draw simple conclusions and answer questions. Use information from secondary sources to help answer a question.

N.B. Any children not hitting *working towards ARE* should come under *below ARE* when recording attainment in Active Learn Primary.

Now you see me, now you don't!

Evolution usually takes thousands of years but there is one example of a species evolving much more quickly.

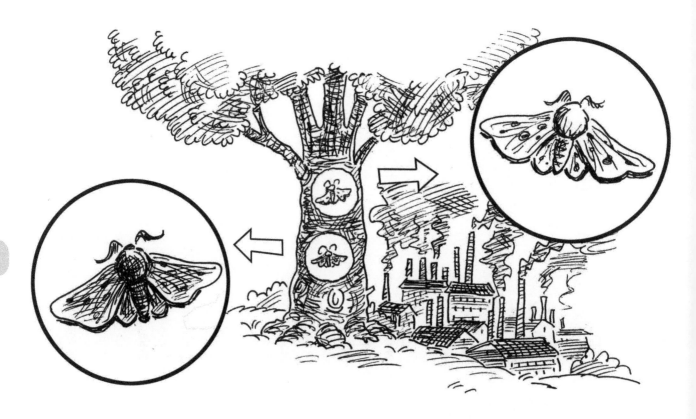

What can you find out about the evolution of the peppered moth?

What you need to do

- Carry out a challenge to model the adaptation of peppered moths.
- Write about how peppered moths adapted to changes in their environment.
- Choose another animal and explain why their adaptation gives them an advantage in its environment.

You may find these words helpful

adapt, adaptation, advantage, survive, environment, natural selection, change, reproduce, camouflage

Name:

Class: _____ **Date:** _____

Peppered moths

How the environment changed in the nineteenth century:

_____

_____

_____

How peppered moths evolved and adapted to their environment:

_____

_____

_____

_____

_____

_____

_____

_____

_____

_____

_____

Explanation of how _____ has evolved to survive in its environment

Another example of animal adaptation is _____

They live: _____

_____

_____

_____

_____ evolved and adapted to their environment by:

_____

_____

_____

_____

_____

_____

_____

_____

For teacher use

What went well	
How to improve	